NATIONAL
GEOGRAPHIC
KiDS

PUZZLE
BOOK

ANIMALS

Published by Collins
An imprint of HarperCollins Publishers
Westerhill Road
Bishopbriggs
Glasgow G64 2QT
www.harpercollins.co.uk

HarperCollins Publishers
1st Floor, Watermarque Building, Ringsend Road, Dublin 4, Ireland

In association with National Geographic Partners, LLC

NATIONAL GEOGRAPHIC and the Yellow Border Design are trademarks of the
National Geographic Society, used under license.

First published 2018

ISBN 978-0-00-826770-4

10 9 8 7 6

Printed in Great Britain by Bell and Bain Ltd, Glasgow

If you would like to comment on any aspect of this book,
please contact us at the above address or online.
natgeokidsbooks.co.uk
collins.reference@harpercollins.co.uk

Paper from responsible sources.

Acknowledgements

Cover images
Shark — 3DMI / Shutterstock.com; Clownfish — stockpix4u /
Shutterstock.com; Frog—Aleksey Stemmer/Shutterstock.com; Bird
—Rosa Jay/Shutterstock.com; Otter—Eric Isselee/Shutterstock.com;
Baby tiger — Anan Kaewkhammul / Shutterstock.com; Sloth —
kungverylucky / Shutterstock.com; Seahorse — Eric Isselee /
Shutterstock.com; Dragonfly — Hintau Aliaksei / Shuttsrstock.com;
Horse—Dmussman/Shutterstock.com

Images in order of appearance
Shark — 3DMI/Shutterstock.com; Baby tiger — Anan Kaewkhammul/
Shutterstock.com; Tiger—jeep2499/Shutterstock.com; Frog—Adam
Gryko / Shutterstock.com; Crocodile — tratong / Shutterstock.com;
Hippo — Wlad74 / Shutterstock.com; Piglet — Richard Peterson /
Shutterstock.com; Meerkat — Rosa Jay/Shutterstock.com; Starfish
—aaltair/Shutterstock.com; Lion roaring — Eric Isselee/Shutterstock.
com; Tiger — Vladimir Wrangel / Shutterstock.com; Panther — David
Newbold/Shutterstock.com; Lynx — Ondrej Prosicky/Shutterstock.
com; Jaguar — Volodymyr Burdiak/Shutterstock.com; Leopard—Eric
Isselee/Shutterstock.com; Snow Leopard—Leeloona/Shutterstock.
com; Cheetah — Arnoud Quanjer / Shutterstock.com; Puma — J. T.
Chapman / Shutterstock.com; Panther — Leonardo Mercon /
Shutterstock.com; Leopard—Matt Porter Wildlife/Shutterstock.com;
Lion — Maggy Meyer / Shutterstock.com; Tiger — konmesa /
Shutterstock.com; Cheetah — Maros Bauer / Shutterstock.com;
Lioness — Eric Isselee / Shutterstock.com; Lion cub — Eric Isselee /
Shutterstock.com; Baby Orangutan—Eric Isselee/Shutterstock.com;
Parrot — Eric Isselee / Shutterstock.com; Sloth — kungverylucky /
Shutterstock.com; Monkey—fontoknak/Shutterstock.com; Tree frog
— Dirk Ercken / Shutterstock.com; Ant — Yaping / Shutterstock.com;
Toucan — Tadas_Jucys / Shutterstock.com; Anaconda — chamleuneja /
Shutterstock.com; Tree frog scene—Vaclav Sebek/Shutterstock.com;
Gorilla — Berendje Photography / Shutterstock.com; Pythons —
cellistka/Shutterstock.com; Iguana — Erik Lam/Shutterstock.com;
Open mouthed crocodile — reptiles4all/Shutterstock.com; Toads —
Hintau Aliakse/Shutterstock.com; Frogs — Smit/Shutterstock.com;
Otter — Eric Isselee / Shutterstock.com; Heron — AngelaLouwe /
Shutterstock.com; Dragonflies—Hintau Aliaksei/Shutterstock.com;
Shoebill—Iues01/Shutterstock.com; Beaver—Jody Ann/Shutterstock.
com; Flamingo—cyo bo/Shutterstock.com; Busy swamp scene—Sergey
Uryadnikov / Shutterstock.com; Snake — PUSCAU DANIEL /
Shutterstock.com; Alligator — nattanan726 / Shutterstock.com;
Giraffe — a_v_d / Shutterstock.com; Elephant — Four Oaks /
Shutterstock.com; Hippos— Eric Isselee/Shutterstock.com; Cheetah
—Eric Isselee/Shutterstock.com; Zebra—prapass/Shutterstock.com;
Vulture — Eric Isselee / Shutterstock.com; Rhino — gualtiero boffi /
Shutterstock.com; Lion — Eric Isselee / Shutterstock.com; Hyena —
Aaron Amat / Shutterstock.com; Gazelle — Marcel Brekelmans /
Shutterstock.com; Giraffe — Pyty/Shutterstock.com; Hippo — Karel
Bartik/Shutterstock.com; Rhino—JONATHAN PLEDGER/Shutterstock.
com; Roller—Johan Swanepoel/Shutterstock.com; Zebra—Eugen Haag
/ Shutterstock.com; Elephant — Martin Gallie / Shutterstock.com;
Gazelle — Sergei25 / Shutterstock.com; Buffalo — 2630ben /
Shutterstock.com; Cow—Dudarev Mikhail/Shutterstock.com; Sheep
—O.M/Shutterstock.com; Chicken—stockphoto mania/Shutterstock.
com; Pig — yevgeniy11/Shutterstock.com; Ducks — JIANG HONGYAN/
Shutterstock.com; Goose—Bildagentur Zoonar GmbH/Shutterstock.
com; Sheep — N-sky / Shutterstock.com; Donkey — Marco Barone /
Shutterstock.com; Goat — Khalangot Sergey L / Shutterstock.com;
Duck — TTstudio / Shutterstock.com; Cow — VanderWolf Images /
Shutterstock.com; Sheep — Jodie Nash / Shutterstock.com; Pig —
Alexander Raths / Shutterstock.com; Horse — Rusla Ruseyn /
Shutterstock.com; Horse—Dmussman/Shutterstock.com; Dog—Runa
Kazakova / Shutterstock.com; Chick — Lapse studio / Shutterstock.
com; Hen—stockphoto mania/Shutterstock.com; Tarsier— Bambara
/ Shutterstock.com; Meerkat — Susan Schmitz / Shutterstock.com;
Gharial—Trevor Fairbank/Shutterstock.com; Mantis Shrimp—Richard
Whitcombe / Shutterstock.com; Pangolin — 2630ben / Shutterstock.
com; Gerenuk — Sergey Uryadnikov / Shutterstock.com; Lowland
Streaked Tenrec — reptiles4all/Shutterstock.com; Porcupine — Eric
Isselee/Shutterstock.com; Tarantula—pets in frames/Shutterstock.
com; Sunda Colugo — Vincent St. Thomas / Shutterstock.com; Busy
meerkat scene—P.Burghardt/Shutterstock.com; Penguin—Christian
Rordam/Shutterstock.com; Jerboa—reptiles4all/Shutterstock.com;
Axolotl — Eric Isselee / Shutterstock.com; Dolphin — ArchMan /
Shutterstock.com; Starfish — Kletr / Shutterstock.com; Octopus—
zhengzaishuru/Shutterstock.com; Seal—Eric Isselee/Shutterstock.
com; Shark — 3DMI / Shutterstock.com; Clownfish — stockpix4u /
Shutterstock.com; Sea turtle — Rich Carey/Shutterstock.com; Sea
Horse — Eric Isselee/Shutterstock.com; Piranha — Andrew Burgess/
Shutterstock.com; Crab—Eric Isselee/Shutterstock.com; Busy under
water scene — Vlad61 / Shutterstock.com; Whale — Mike Price /
Shutterstock.com; Penguin — javarman / Shutterstock.com; Beaver
—Oleksandr Lytvynenko/Shutterstock.com

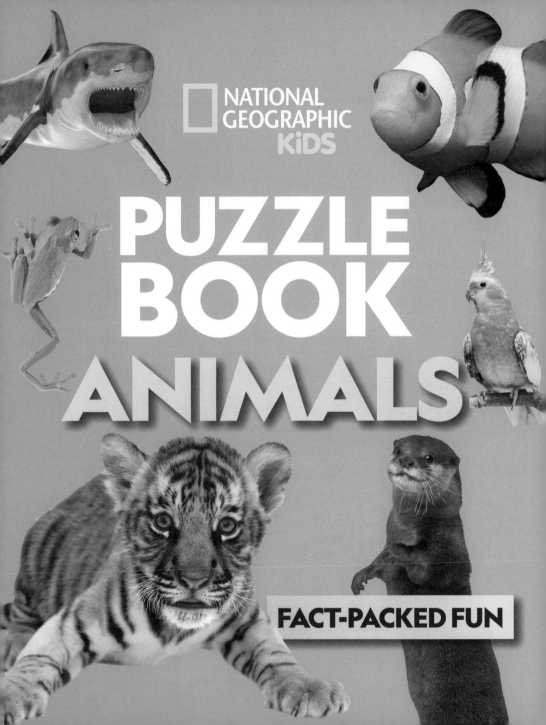

NATIONAL GEOGRAPHIC KiDS

PUZZLE BOOK

ANIMALS

FACT-PACKED FUN

CONTENTS

Big cats

Are you brave enough for fun facts and puzzles about big cats? Read on to find out more.

A LION'S MIGHTY ROAR is so LOUD it can be heard up to 8 KM AWAY!

CROSSWORDS

Help the big cats fill in the crosswords by solving the cryptic clues below.
Answers have the same amount of letters as the number in brackets.
Can you work out the big cat using the letters in the shaded squares?
See if you are right by flicking to page 90.

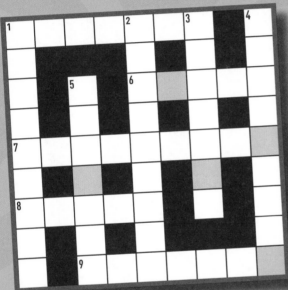

EVERY TIGER in the **WORLD** has a completely **UNIQUE STRIPE PATTERN.**

Across
1. Small wild flowers with white petals (7)
6. Tiny piece of bread (5)
7. Of great significance (9)
8. Brother of your father or mother (5)
9. A leafy green vegetable (7)

Down
1. Hard (9)
2. Not right (9)
3. Part of a hot dog (7)
4. Material; anagram of 'cuts beans' (9)
5. Normal and usual (7)

Some **PANTHERS** are actually just **BLACK LEOPARDS**, so they still have **SPOTS**, but they're much **HARDER TO SEE.**

Across
1   Small red fruit with a hard stone (6)
6   Nine plus eight (9)
7   Birds of prey that hoot (4)
8   Create (4)
9   The opposite of cheap (9)
11 Road (6)

Down
1   Person who buys something in a shop (8)
2   You put a letter in this before posting it (8)
3   Sprint (3)
4   A sister or uncle, for instance (8)
5   Excite the curiosity of someone (8)
10 Food for a squirrel (3)

SUDOKUS

Help the big cats crack the sudokus. Fill in the blank squares so that numbers 1 to 6 appear once in each row, column and 3x2 box. See if you are right by flicking to page 90.

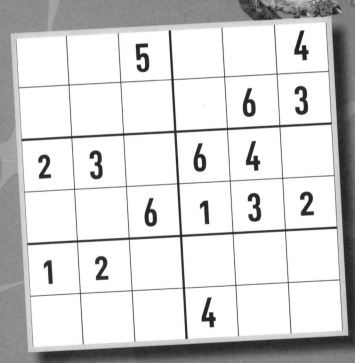

LYNX are **STEALTHY, MYSTERIOUS** creatures and are **RARELY SEEN** by **HUMANS.**

		5			4
				6	3
2	3		6	4	
		6	1	3	2
1	2				
			4		

4	3			5	2
		1			
			5		4
1		5			
			3		
2	1	3		6	5

Unlike most cats,
JAGUARS LIKE WATER and
are **VERY GOOD SWIMMERS.**

	2		3	1	
					5
	4	2	6		
		3		2	
2					
3	5	1		6	2

Wordsearches

Can you find the words relating to big cats?
Search left to right; up and down to find the words listed in the boxes below.
See if you are right by flicking to page 90.

cheetah	puma
jaguar	roar
leopard	spots
lion	stripes
panther	tiger

LEOPARDS are **GREAT CLIMBERS,** and sometimes like to rest **HIGH UP IN THE TREES.**

e	k	e	s	u	w	g	f	e	s
x	d	a	g	j	a	g	u	a	r
o	a	w	s	p	s	p	o	t	s
o	p	u	m	a	t	r	l	r	e
y	l	i	o	n	r	a	e	e	l
u	a	k	t	t	i	r	o	a	r
z	z	k	o	h	p	t	p	s	s
s	v	c	h	e	e	t	a	h	a
t	i	g	e	r	s	a	r	w	e
a	x	b	p	l	j	i	d	c	s

SNOW LEOPARDS have **BIG, WIDE, FURRY FEET** that act like **NATURAL SNOWSHOES.**

w	a	u	x	l	m	u	p	b	g
r	q	c	o	u	g	a	r	s	h
a	g	a	t	a	t	s	p	g	g
o	p	r	e	d	a	t	o	r	t
p	r	n	e	s	c	e	u	i	s
t	e	i	t	o	l	a	n	c	a
i	y	v	h	w	a	l	c	z	r
t	l	o	f	m	w	t	e	m	o
c	y	r	u	d	s	h	i	h	r
f	i	e	r	c	e	a	w	i	a

carnivore

claws

cougar

fierce

fur

pounce

predator

prey

stealth

teeth

CLOSE UP

Match the mind-boggling magnifications of big cats to the named pictures opposite. See if you are right by flicking to page 91.

1

2
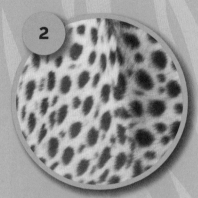

3

4

5

6

Cheetah 1

Puma 2

Panther 3

Leopard 4

Lion 5

Tiger 6

GUESS WHAT?

Can you guess the answers to the big cat questions below?
Check your guesses by flicking to page 91.

1. Which big cat is known as the 'king of the jungle'?
   a) Elephant
   b) Lion
   c) Hyena

2. Leopards are known for their:
   a) Bark
   b) Stripes
   c) Spots

3. Which big cat is also known as a mountain lion?
   a) Puma
   b) Donkey
   c) Ocelot

4. Which is the fastest animal on land?
   a) Lion
   b) Cheetah
   c) Tiger

5. Why do snow leopards have very large paws?
   a) To jump higher
   b) To use tools
   c) To help distribute their weight when walking on snow

6. If a male lion and female tiger breed they produce a:
   a) Tigeron
   b) Liger
   c) Lionger

7. Which is the largest cat species?
   a) Lion
   b) Jaguar
   c) Tiger

8. Lions live together in a group known as a:
   a) Team
   b) Flock
   c) Pride

9. A jaguar's preferred habitat is:
   a) Dense rainforest
   b) The Sahara Desert
   c) Sea

10. An adult lion's roar can be heard:
    a) 50 metres away
    b) 8 kilometres away
    c) 50 miles away

Help the lioness around the maze to find her cub.
See if you are right by flicking to page 91.

MAZE

Word wheels

Can you work out the big cats
in the two word wheels?

See if you are right by flicking to page 91.

In the jungle

Swing through this chapter to find fun facts and puzzles from the jungle.

Look familiar? The **ORANGUTAN** is one of our **CLOSEST RELATIVES** – we have nearly 97 % **OF THE SAME DNA!**

CROSSWORDS

Help the jungle animals fill in the crosswords by solving the cryptic clues below.
Answers have the same amount of letters as the number in brackets.
Can you work out the jungle animals using the letters in the shaded squares?
See if you are right by flicking to page 92.

There are more than **350 DIFFERENT PARROT SPECIES** in the **WORLD.**

Across
1 The first meal of the day (9)
4 Pudding (7)
6 Place where bees live (7)
9 Sour liquid put on chips (7)
10 Say sorry (9)

Down
1 People sleep in these (4)
2 Pardon; excuse (7)
3 The end parts of the feet (4)
5 Better or more important than other things (7)
7 Large American wild cat also known as a cougar (4)
8 A woody plant such as an oak or sycamore (4)

Across

1 Orange vegetables (7)
6 Not liked (9)
8 The person that lives next door to you (9)
9 One more (7)

Down

2 Creature like a frog or toad (9)
3 Device used to study stars (9)
4 The opposite of pulling (7)
5 Authors (7)
7 Juicy yellowish-pink fruit (5)

SUDOKUS

Help the jungle animals crack the sudokus. Fill in the blank squares so that numbers 1 to 6 appear once in each row, column and 3x2 box.
See if you are right by flicking to page 92.

	6				
2		5	6		3
			2		
6		4			
1	3	2	5		4
4				3	

The **WORLD** is home to over **10,000 SPECIES** of **ANTS.**

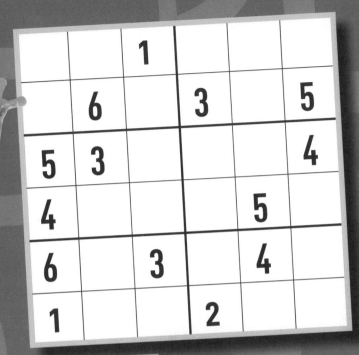

Top puzzle:

		1			
	6		3		5
5	3				4
4				5	
6		3		4	
1			2		

Bottom puzzle:

	4		1		
					5
5		2		3	4
6	3		5		
2					
4		3		6	

A **TREE FROG'S NEON COLOURS** may **SHOCK** and **CONFUSE** predators, allowing the frog to **JUMP AWAY.**

Wordsearches

Can you find the words relating to jungle animals?
Search left to right, up and down to find the words listed in the boxes below.
See if you are right by flicking to page 92.

bushbaby
chameleon
cobra
crocodile
macaw

ocelot
orangutan
panther
piranha
tapir

One of the **MOST COLOURFUL** types of **TOUCAN** is the **KEEL-BILLED**, or **'RAINBOW-BILLED'**, toucan.

a	g	s	c	o	c	e	l	o	t
q	o	t	p	a	n	t	h	e	r
c	r	o	c	o	d	i	l	e	p
b	u	s	h	b	a	b	y	j	i
r	p	a	y	e	t	a	p	i	r
t	s	a	y	n	r	b	x	t	a
t	o	r	a	n	g	u	t	a	n
r	l	m	a	c	a	w	s	z	h
t	o	j	a	v	c	o	b	r	a
x	c	h	a	m	e	l	e	o	n

i m b a t o u c a n
l l a x p h m h g e
m v a e y i l i o n
q y o l t x x m r t
q t p q h u o p i d
a n a c o n d a l u
s l r f n a r n l o
y f r o g a r z a a
s l o t h i s e i p
i s t f o e i e p s

GREEN ANACONDAS are the **LARGEST** and **HEAVIEST SNAKES** in the world.

anaconda
bat
chimpanzee
frog
gorilla

lion
parrot
python
sloth
toucan

Compare the two images of the tree frog.
Can you spot the five differences between the images?
See if you are right by flicking to page 93.

See if you are right by flicking to page 93.

TREE FROGS have an EXTRA EYELID that they can use to help them SEE UNDERWATER.

GUESS WHAT?

Can you guess the answers to the jungle animal questions below?
Check your guesses by flicking to page 93.

1. Which jungle creature can mimic the human voice?
   a) Chimpanzee
   b) Parrot
   c) Snake

2. Which animal is the largest living primate?
   a) Baboon
   b) Gorilla
   c) Chimpanzee

3. The sloth is known for being extremely:
   a) Fast
   b) Slow
   c) Tall

4. How many species of snake exist in the world?
   a) 35
   b) 350
   c) More than 3,500

5. Termites live in large groups called:
   a) Palaces
   b) Colonies
   c) Kingdoms

6. What are toucans well-known for?
   a) Their massive beaks
   b) Their ability to talk
   c) Their ability to hover

7. What are the largest and heaviest snakes in the workd?
   a) Green anacondas
   b) Black anacondas
   c) Red anacondas

8. What is a tapir?
   a) A type of lizard
   b) A hoofed mammal
   c) A tropical fish

9. Which of these snakes is venomous?
   a) Cobra
   b) Python
   c) Grass snake

10. The average lifespan of a chimpanzee in the wild is:
    a) 5 years
    b) 20 years
    c) 45 years

Help the snake around the maze until it finds the exit.
See if you are right by flicking to page 93.

MAZE

Word wheels

Can you work out the jungle animals
in the two word wheels?
See if you are right by flicking to page 93.

Word wheel 1: A L O G R I L (center: G)

Word wheel 2: P I R H N A A (center: H)

Swamps and wetlands

Make your way through this section to discover fun facts and puzzles on swamps and wetlands.

CROCODILES as we know them today have been on **EARTH** for around 80 **MILLION YEARS!**

CROSSWORDS

Help the swamp animals fill in the crosswords by solving the cryptic clues below.
Answers have the same amount of letters as the number in brackets.
Can you work out the swamp animal using the letters in the shaded squares?
See if you are right by flicking to page 94.

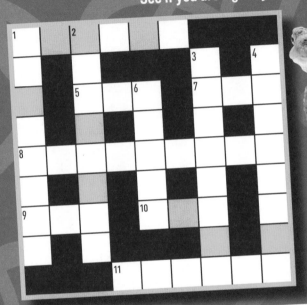

In 1935, **3,000 CANE TOADS** were released in **AUSTRALIA** – now there are over **200 MILLION** there.

Across
1 Straight; credit (anagram) (6)
5 A young bear or lion (3)
7 Sprinted (3)
8 You might spread this on toast (9)
9 Organ you see with (3)
10 Animal that barks (3)
11 Opposite of oldest (6)

Down
1 Last month of the year (8)
2 Simple musical instrument (8)
3 Shape with three sides (8)
4 Global computer network you use to visit websites (8)
6 Facial hair (5)

RIVER OTTERS are very playful, they love to **SLIDE DOWN MUDDY** or **SNOWY HILLS** for fun.

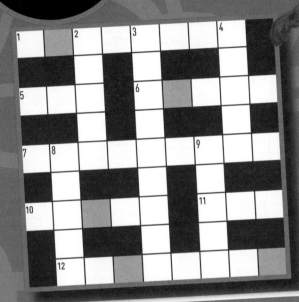

Across

1 Ball game you might play at school (8)
5 Weird or strange; not even (3)
6 Water vapour (5)
7 Flying vehicle (9)
10 Have the same opinion about something (5)
11 How old you are (3)
12 Way in (8)

Down

2 Beneath (5)
3 Vanish from sight (9)
4 A dirty mark on clothes (5)
8 Impressive bird of prey (5)
9 Once more (5)

SUDOKUS

Help the swamp animals crack the sudokus. Fill in the blank squares so that numbers 1 to 6 appear once in each row, column and 3x2 box.
See if you are right by flicking to page 94.

			6		2
		3		4	
4		6			3
2			1		4
3	5		4		
1		4			

HERONS
are **EXPERT FISHERS**, and usually **EAT FISH** by **SWALLOWING THEM WHOLE!**

				1	
3			4		2
6	3	5			
			5	6	
5		3			1
4	1	6			

		3		4	2
	4		3	5	
6			2		
		2			5
		5		3	
	6		5		

Wordsearches

Can you find the words relating to swamps and wetlands?
Search left to right, up and down to find the words listed in the boxes below.
See if you are right by flicking to page 94.

A **BEAVER'S FUR** is **OILY** and **NATURALLY WATERPROOF**, which keeps the skin underneath **NICE AND DRY.**

l	p	u	c	r	a	n	e	h	e
o	m	a	r	s	h	r	u	d	p
j	x	m	o	n	e	l	a	r	x
t	i	a	c	a	t	c	r	a	b
u	b	b	o	k	f	r	o	g	g
z	i	v	d	e	k	e	r	o	o
d	j	l	i	z	a	r	d	n	t
v	r	d	l	a	l	l	o	f	t
u	c	b	e	t	u	r	t	l	e
p	t	w	d	g	t	s	k	y	r

crab
crane
crocodile
dragonfly
frog

lizard
marsh
otter
snake
turtle

l	y	a	b	u	r	t	w	c	s
m	r	d	e	h	y	b	w	r	h
a	z	u	a	e	f	l	h	a	r
n	e	c	v	r	l	a	c	y	i
g	c	k	e	o	a	c	p	f	m
r	a	s	r	n	m	k	f	i	p
o	i	i	g	a	i	b	r	s	y
v	m	l	u	i	n	e	a	h	m
e	a	l	l	i	g	a	t	o	r
u	n	t	s	q	o	r	c	q	e

FLAMINGOS are **BORN GREY** but gradually turn pink because of a **DYE IN THE SHRIMP** that they eat.

alligator
beaver
black bear
caiman
crayfish

duck
flamingo
heron
mangrove
shrimp

SPOT THE DIFFERENCE

Compare the two images of the crocodiles.
Can you spot the five differences between the images?
See if you are right by flicking to page 95.

CASSIUS, the oldest known crocodile in the world, is over **110 YEARS OLD.**

GUESS WHAT?

Can you guess the answers to the swamp and wetland animal questions below?
Check your guesses by flicking to page 95.

1. Which enormous snake lives in South American swamps?
   a) Anaconda
   b) Adder
   c) Grass snake

2. Which of these is a type of bird?
   a) Crane
   b) Tractor
   c) Van

3. Which of these is a type of duck?
   a) Buzzard
   b) Leotard
   c) Mallard

4. Beavers are known for:
   a) Eating meat
   b) Building dams
   c) Climbing mountains

5. Which of the following is a rodent?
   a) Newt
   b) Snail
   c) Rat

6. Which of these creatures walks sideways?
   a) Giraffe
   b) Dog
   c) Crab

7. Why do dragonflies dip their tails into water?
   a) To drink
   b) To lay eggs
   c) To test the water temperature

8. Which of these is a type of wetland?
   a) Bog
   b) Meadow
   c) Prairie

9. Which plant might you find in a pond?
   a) Water lily
   b) Cactus
   c) Rose

10. What is the larva of a frog called?
    a) Tadpole
    b) Maypole
    c) Flagpole

Help the crocodile around the
maze until it finds the exit.
See if you are right by flicking to page 95.

M A Z E

Word wheels

Can you work out the swamp animals
in the two word wheels?
See if you are right by flicking to page 95.

Word wheel 1: T R L A A O G L I

Word wheel 2: T T E R L U

On safari

Buckle up and keep your eyes peeled in this chapter for fun facts and puzzles about safari animals.

GIRAFFES give **BIRTH STANDING UP,** which means **NEWBORN CALVES** drop **1.5 METRES** to the ground.

CROSSWORDS

Help the safari animals fill in the crosswords by solving the cryptic clues below.
Answers have the same amount of letters as the number in brackets.
Can you work out the safari animal using the letters in the shaded squares?
See if you are right by flicking to page 96.

Across
1 An entertainer who performs gymnastic feats (7)
6 Slippery snake-like fish (3)
8 Time of day before you go to bed (7)
9 Large African ape (7)
10 Nine plus one (3)
11 Large cat also known as a panther (7)

Down
2 Acknowledge a significant date such as your birthday (9)
3 Large reptile (9)
4 Shape with six sides (7)
5 Where one finds London (7)
7 Respond (5)

ELEPHANTS can be pregnant for up to **22 MONTHS** before their babies are born – that's a long wait!

HIPPOS can fold their **EARS** and **NOSTRILS SHUT** underwater, and hold their breath for up to **FIVE MINUTES.**

Across

1 Become less (8)
5 Selected (5)
7 Yellow citrus fruit (5)
8 House made of solid snow (5)
9 Very odd; strange (5)
10 Animals that pull Santa's sleigh (8)

Down

1 Choice or selection (8)
2 Hot ___ : sweet cocoa drink (9)
3 Ship that goes underwater (9)
4 Think carefully about (8)
6 Arm joint (5)

SUDOKUS

Help the safari animals crack the sudokus. Fill in the blank squares so that numbers 1 to 6 appear once in each row, column and 3x2 box.
See if you are right by flicking to page 96.

Despite many theories, **SCIENTISTS** still aren't completely sure **WHY ZEBRAS HAVE STRIPES.**

			6		
1	4			5	
3	5		2	6	4
	6	2			5
				2	3
		3			

VULTURES are the **RUBBISH COLLECTORS** of the animal world, cleaning up the mess by eating animals that have died.

	3		1	6	2
			5		
1		5			3
3			4		5
		1	3		
6		3			

4	1	5			
		2	4		
		4		5	
	5		2		
		6	5		
5		1		2	4

Wordsearches

Can you find the words relating to safari animals?
Search left to right, up and down to find the words listed in the boxes below.
See if you are right by flicking to page 96.

e	j	a	c	k	a	l	s	m	g
d	r	r	w	i	l	d	d	o	g
q	r	b	x	b	k	s	j	n	s
f	h	a	o	z	g	r	t	g	o
b	y	b	o	r	o	l	p	o	s
p	e	o	o	l	r	p	h	o	t
r	n	o	y	a	i	j	c	s	r
r	a	n	t	e	l	o	p	e	i
a	g	a	z	e	l	l	e	l	c
i	m	p	a	l	a	t	q	p	h

antelope

baboon

gazelle

gorilla

hyena

impala

jackal

mongoose

ostrich

wild dog

48

SPOTTED HYENAS are also known as **'LAUGHING HYENAS'**, because they **CACKLE LOUDLY** to communicate.

buffalo
cheetah
crocodile
elephant
giraffe

leopard
lion
rhinoceros
warthog
zebra

LIONS usually only live on **GRASS PLAINS,** so they aren't really **'KING OF THE JUNGLE'** after all.

y	h	l	a	r	l	r	q	r	w
r	t	c	h	e	e	t	a	h	a
i	x	a	l	i	o	n	z	i	r
a	b	e	l	e	p	h	a	n	t
c	z	e	b	r	a	t	u	o	h
f	b	f	l	r	r	o	o	c	o
c	r	o	c	o	d	i	l	e	g
g	i	r	a	f	f	e	y	r	y
p	r	b	u	f	f	a	l	o	a
p	i	o	t	h	v	s	t	s	t

CLOSE UP

Match the mind-boggling magnifications of safari animals to the named pictures opposite. See if you are right by flicking to page 97.

1
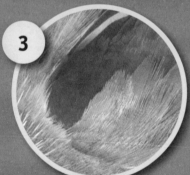

2
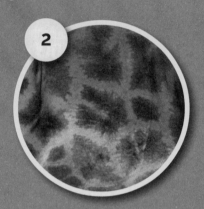

3

4

5

6

Gazelle

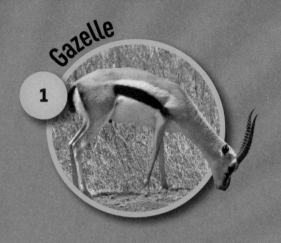

1

Giraffe

2

Hippo

3

Rhino

4

Roller

5

6

Zebra

GUESS WHAT?

Can you guess the answers to the safari animal questions below?
Check your guesses by flicking to page 97.

1. Which animal is famous for being striped?
   a) Zebra
   b) Bear
   c) Lion

2. How long is a giraffe's tongue?
   a) 5 cm
   b) 52 cm
   c) 90 cm

3. What is a male elephant called?
   a) Buck
   b) Boar
   c) Bull

4. Which safari animal is known for its 'laugh'?
   a) Spotted tiger
   b) Spotted hyena
   c) Spotted warthog

5. How many species of baboons are there?
   a) One
   b) Five
   c) Nine

6. African wild dogs are:
   a) Canines
   b) Felines
   c) Reptiles

7. A gazelle is a type of:
   a) Antelope
   b) Ant
   c) Elephant

8. Which animal name rhymes with the word 'smile'?
   a) Lion
   b) Zebra
   c) Crocodile

9. Unlike other big cats, which animal hunts mainly during the day?
   a) Lion
   b) Leopard
   c) Cheetah

10. Warthog tusks can grow up to approximately how long?
    a) 25 cm
    b) 75 cm
    c) 95 cm

Help the gazelle around the maze
until it finds the exit.
See if you are right by flicking to page 97.

O F
B **F** L
A U

L E
Z **L** A
G E

Word wheels

Can you work out the safari animals
in the two word wheels?
See if you are right by flicking to page 97.

At the farm

Read on for fun facts and puzzles from down at the farm.

COW'S STOMACHS are **DIVIDED INTO FOUR 'CHAMBERS'**, allowing them to **DIGEST GRASS** and **GRAINS** better.

CROSSWORDS

Help the farm animals fill in the crosswords by solving the cryptic clues below.
Answers have the same amount of letters as the number in brackets.
Can you work out the farm word using the letters in the shaded squares?
See if you are right by flicking to page 98.

Across

1 Very impressive or incredible (9)
5 Type of vehicle (3)
7 Illustration; typical case (7)
8 Frequent (7)
11 The whole of (3)
12 Crisis (9)

Down

1 Best-loved (9)
2 Zero (4)
3 Stumble (4)
4 Cautiously (9)
6 Furniture item with a flat top (5)
9 Donate (4)
10 Drizzle, perhaps (4)

PIGS don't have working **SWEAT GLANDS.** Instead, they use **WATER** or **MUD** to **STAY COOL** in hot weather.

Across
4 Country (6)
6 A single time (4)
7 Possess (3)
8 Animals that moo (4)
9 Large white waterbird (4)
10 A large primate (3)
11 List of food items at a restaurant (4)
12 Outcome (6)

Down
1 Trick-or-treating happens on this day (9)
2 Tyrannosaurus rex, for example (8)
3 Oblong (9)
5 Rubbish (8)

The **CHICKEN** is the **CLOSEST** living **RELATIVE** to the great **TYRANNOSAURUS REX.**

SUDOKUS

Help the farm animals crack the sudokus. Fill in the blank squares so that numbers 1 to 6 appear once in each row, column and 3x2 box. See if you are right by flicking to page 98.

3		5			
				6	3
2	3		6		
		6		3	2
1	2				
6			4		

Only **FEMALE DUCKS** actually **'QUACK'**, but all ducks **GRUNT, YODEL** and **WHISTLE.**

4	3	6		5	2
		1			
			5		4
1		5			
			3		
2				6	5

4	2	5	3	1	
					5
	4		6		
		3		2	
2					
	5	1		6	2

A group of **GEESE** can be called a **'GAGGLE'** on the ground, a **'SKEIN'** in flight, and a **'FLOCK'** anywhere.

59

Wordsearches

Can you find the words relating to farm animals?
Search left to right, up and down to find the words listed in the boxes below.
See if you are right by flicking to page 98.

b	r	n	c	y	t	t	e	r	d
x	c	l	n	a	c	r	c	o	w
w	h	r	e	m	k	a	h	b	g
g	o	a	t	a	s	c	i	d	o
c	r	a	b	b	i	t	c	u	o
s	s	f	a	g	m	o	k	c	s
l	e	u	r	p	a	r	e	k	e
t	t	a	n	m	s	p	n	z	u
l	o	s	h	e	e	p	m	a	v
v	m	g	g	z	s	c	f	m	w

barn

chicken

cow

duck

goat

goose

horse

rabbit

sheep

tractor

crops

dog

donkey

farmer

hay bales

lamb

pig

plough

rooster

stables

p	i	g	c	l	z	x	m	c	d
p	f	a	r	m	e	r	t	u	o
l	s	d	o	g	s	o	u	s	n
o	b	v	p	q	t	o	r	h	k
u	s	e	s	j	a	s	s	b	e
g	k	j	v	l	b	t	l	u	y
h	a	y	b	a	l	e	s	q	t
c	r	x	u	m	e	r	l	w	l
q	d	d	r	b	s	i	s	a	e
h	t	l	l	y	u	i	p	a	e

CLOSE UP

Match the mind-boggling magnifications of farm animals to the named pictures opposite. See if you are right by flicking to page 99.

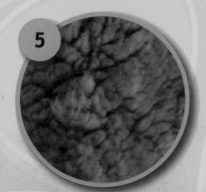

1

2

3

4

5

6

Goat
1

Duck
2

Cow
3

Sheep
4

Pig
5

Horse
6

63

GUESS WHAT?

Can you guess the answers to the farm animal questions below?
Check your guesses by flicking to page 99.

1. Which animal is well-known for its loud morning call?
   a) Rooster
   b) Sheep
   c) Cow

2. A group of geese are called a:
   a) Pack
   b) Skein
   c) Herd

3. Which animal grazes in a flock?
   a) Sheep
   b) Rabbit
   c) Dog

4. Which bird lays eggs and lives in a coop?
   a) Chicken
   b) Swan
   c) Parrot

5. Which animal helps to herd and control sheep?
   a) Sheepdog
   b) Horse
   c) Pig

6. Horses sleep in a:
   a) Farmhouse
   b) Coop
   c) Stable

7. Farmers sheer wool from:
   a) Horse
   b) Chickens
   c) Sheep

8. A baby cow is called a:
   a) Cub
   b) Calf
   c) Piglet

9. A young sheep is called a:
   a) Kitten
   b) Puppy
   c) Lamb

10. A female donkey is called:
   a) Jenny
   b) Jackie
   c) Joyce

Help the hen around the maze to reach her chick. See if you are right by flicking to page 99.

MAZE

Word wheels

R B
A I B
T

K N
Y
E D
O

Can you work out the farm animals
in the two word wheels?
See if you are right by flicking to page 99.

Curious creatures

Eager to learn more about our fascinating friends? Read on for fun facts and puzzles about curious creatures.

TARSIERS have the nickname 'FOREST GOBLINS' because of their **TINY SIZE** and **FUNNY APPEARANCE**.

CROSSWORDS

Help the curious creatures fill in the crosswords by solving the cryptic clues below.
Answers have the same amount of letters as the number in brackets.
Can you work out the curious creature using the letters in the shaded squares?
See if you are right by flicking to page 100.

Each **MEERKAT MOB** has at least one **'SENTRY'**, that **STANDS UP ON ITS HIND LEGS** to look out for danger.

Across
4 Very clever or talented (9)
6 Adult males (3)
8 Large number of people (5)
9 Tube you can drink through (5)
10 Crafty and cunning (3)
12 Place in a school where lessons take place (9)

Down
1 Opposite of false (4)
2 The direction the hands on a watch move (9)
3 Very well-known (6)
5 This comes after yesterday and before tomorrow (5)
6 Melodic sounds (5)
7 Ordinary; regular (6)
11 Big cat that roars (4)

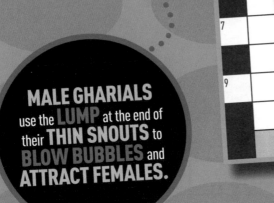

MALE GHARIALS use the **LUMP** at the end of their **THIN SNOUTS** to **BLOW BUBBLES** and **ATTRACT FEMALES.**

Across

4 Thrill (6)
6 The opposite of win (4)
7 Too (4)
8 Remove the skin from a fruit (4)
9 Where you are right now (4)
10 What an aeroplane takes off from (6)

Down

1 Very good (9)
2 Find or locate (8)
3 The day before today (9)
5 Large mammal with a trunk (8)

SUDOKUS

Help the curious creatures crack the sudokus. Fill in the blank squares so that numbers 1 to 6 appear once in each row, column and 3x2 box.
See if you are right by flicking to page 100.

PANGOLINS are
SHY CREATURES
that CURL UP
INTO A BALL
when they FEEL
THREATENED.

4		6	3		1
				5	
	4		2		3
6		2		4	
	6				
3			4		

GERENUKS are sometimes called **'GIRAFFE GAZELLES'** because of their **LONG, THIN NECKS.**

LOWLAND STREAKED TENRECS, endemic to **MADAGASCAR,** rub their spines together to **COMMUNICATE.**

Grid 1:

				1	2
			4	3	6
6	2				5
4					
5	3	2			
1	4				

Grid 2:

5		4			1
	3	2			
		3			
			5		4
			6	4	3
3			2		5

Wordsearches

Can you find the words relating to curious creatures?
Search left to right, up and down to find the words listed in the boxes below.
See if you are right by flicking to page 100.

anteater
hermit crab
mole
otter
porcupine

scorpion
shark
skunk
sponge
tarantula

COLUGOS
are forest-dwelling animals
that live in **ASIA.** Flaps
of skin between their legs
allow them to **GLIDE** as
they **LEAP** between
trees.

Known for being
**PRICKLY,
PORCUPINES**
are first born with
SOFT SPIKES,
which harden over a
few days.

n	t	z	p	z	a	s	g	t	s
h	e	r	m	i	t	c	r	a	b
a	o	i	n	x	s	o	r	r	f
n	s	h	a	r	k	r	u	a	i
t	p	o	r	c	u	p	i	n	e
e	o	t	l	u	n	i	v	t	e
a	n	t	t	j	k	o	l	u	y
t	g	e	o	q	h	n	a	l	s
e	e	r	v	s	r	c	s	a	r
r	n	m	m	o	l	e	e	s	j

u	h	r	f	i	t	r	e	z	m
a	t	b	s	n	h	q	l	p	b
v	h	a	x	a	i	m	n	e	s
o	d	d	a	v	t	q	p	n	o
w	o	l	f	a	k	e	e	g	i
l	l	e	m	u	r	a	a	u	b
g	p	a	n	d	a	a	c	i	s
c	h	a	m	e	l	e	o	n	q
l	i	o	s	t	r	i	c	h	t
l	n	p	m	e	e	r	k	a	t

chameleon

dolphin

lemur

meerkat

ostrich

owl

panda

peacock

penguin

wolf

73

SPOT THE DIFFERENCE

Compare the two images of the meerkats.
Can you spot the five differences between the images?
See if you are right by flicking to page 101.

See if you are right by flicking to page 101.

MEERKATS are **SOCIAL ANIMALS,** their mobs can have up to **50 MEMBERS,** and they always **WORK TOGETHER.**

GUESS WHAT?

Can you guess the answers to the curious creature questions below?
Check your guesses by flicking to page 101.

1. Which animal has an ability to change colour?
   a) Chameleon
   b) Tarantula
   c) Panda

2. On which island do you find lemurs in the wild?
   a) Madagascar
   b) Iceland
   c) Ireland

3. Why do stick insects resemble sticks?
   a) To attract a mate
   b) To make it hard for predators to detect them
   c) To keep cool

4. What is a porcupine particularly known for?
   a) Its big teeth
   b) Its sharp spines
   c) Its orange eyes

5. How does a skunk defend itself from predators?
   a) Emits a foul-smelling spray
   b) Jumping up and down
   c) Hides in a shell

6. How do anteaters feed on small insects?
   a) Using their sticky tongues
   b) Scooping them up in their large paws
   c) Sweeping them up with their tails

7. Roughly, how many species of tarantula are known to exist?
   a) 8
   b) 80
   c) 800

8. How long can an otter remain under water?
   a) Up to four seconds
   b) Up to four minutes
   c) Up to forty minutes

9. What do pandas feed on almost entirely?
   a) Oats
   b) Worms
   c) Bamboo

10. Meerkats prefer to live:
    a) Alone
    b) In groups
    c) In pairs

MAZE

Help the jerboa around the maze until it finds the exit. See if you are right by flicking to page 101.

Although **AXOLOTL** are known as **'WALKING FISH'**, they are actually **AMPHIBIANS.**

Word wheels

Can you work out the curious creatures in the two word wheels? See if you are right by flicking to page 101.

In the water

Dive in and discover fun facts and puzzles from under the water.

DOLPHINS COMMUNICATE in lots of different ways, including **BODY LANGUAGE, WHISTLES, AND SQUEAKS.**

CROSSWORDS

Help the sea animals fill in the crosswords by solving the cryptic clues below.
Answers have the same amount of letters as the number in brackets.
Can you work out the sea animal using the letters in the shaded squares?
See if you are right by flicking to page 102.

STARFISH aren't really fish! They actually belong to the same family as **SEA URCHINS** and **SPONGES.**

Across
1. Hug (6)
5. 2 + 3, for instance (3)
7. Road vehicle (3)
8. Bright flash that is followed by thunder (9)
9. Observe with your eyes (3)
10. Tell an untruth (3)
11. A young cat (6)

Down
1. Not giving enough attention to a task (8)
2. Have a different opinion to another (8)
3. Chance event that may lead to injury (8)
4. Scare (8)
6. Gold or iron, for instance (5)

An **OCTOPUS** can use its **EIGHT STRONG ARMS** to build itself a den, complete with a closeable **ROCK 'DOOR'**.

Across

1 Length of space between two points (8)
5 You hear with this (3)
6 Polar ___ : powerful white animals (5)
7 Necklaces and rings, for instance (9)
10 Female monarch (5)
11 Rodent with a long tail (3)
12 Jointly (8)

Down

2 Small mammal that is mouse-like and has a long snout (5)
3 Emergency vehicle (9)
4 Mistake (5)
8 What an active volcano might do (5)
9 Planet we live on (5)

SUDOKUS

Help the sea animals crack the sudokus. Fill in the blank squares so that numbers 1 to 6 appear once in each row, column and 3x2 box.
See if you are right by flicking to page 102.

Thanks to their **POWERFUL TAILS, GREAT WHITE SHARKS** can **SWIM** at up to **60 KM PER HOUR!**

3	5		4		
2		6	3	1	
	1		6	4	2
		1		2	4

Wordsearches

Can you find the words relating to sea animals?
Search left to right, up and down to find the words listed in the boxes below.
See if you are right by flicking to page 102.

coral
jellyfish
octopus
salmon
sardine

seahorse
seaweed
squid
starfish
trout

o	t	r	s	q	u	i	d	k	f
j	s	t	a	r	f	i	s	h	t
j	e	l	l	y	f	i	s	h	u
s	a	r	d	i	n	e	m	u	a
a	h	q	g	x	i	b	r	w	p
l	o	c	t	o	p	u	s	b	o
m	r	r	t	r	o	u	t	t	p
o	s	e	a	w	e	e	d	s	t
n	e	l	l	s	j	h	l	e	h
x	i	u	z	r	c	o	r	a	l

Though **FEMALE SEAHORSES LAY THE EGGS,** it's the males that actually carry them and **'GIVE BIRTH'.**

r	c	f	p	j	s	t	g	t	u
p	s	r	o	e	l	u	r	o	p
g	h	i	i	e	r	n	s	y	i
g	a	l	l	i	g	a	t	o	r
t	r	o	o	a	x	r	u	g	a
x	k	b	e	a	v	e	r	r	n
i	o	s	o	t	c	e	t	v	h
o	u	t	x	y	r	e	l	p	a
l	k	e	w	h	a	l	e	g	j
l	r	r	t	z	b	p	h	u	f

Once a year on **CHRISTMAS ISLAND, MILLIONS OF RED CRABS** travel together from the **FOREST TO THE SEA.**

alligator

beaver

crab

eel

lobster

piranha

shark

tuna

turtle

whale

SPOT THE DIFFERENCE

Compare the two images of the coral reef.
Can you spot the five differences between the images?
See if you are right by flicking to page 103.

See if you are right by flicking to page 103.

CORAL REEFS aren't just plants that are home to thousands of **COLOURFUL FISH,** they are actually living animals themselves!

GUESS WHAT?

Can you guess the answers to the water animal questions below?
Check your guesses by flicking to page 103.

1. How fast can the great white shark swim?
   a) 35 mph
   b) 10 mph
   c) 50 mph

2. How many arms does an octopus have?
   a) Four
   b) Six
   c) Eight

3. The giant squid can grow as long as:
   a) 1 metre
   b) 5 metres
   c) 13 metres

4. How many arms does a starfish have?
   a) Two
   b) Five
   c) Ten

5. What type of creature is a turtle?
   a) Amphibian
   b) Mammal
   c) Reptile

6. A great white shark can grow up to approximately what length?
   a) 1 metre
   b) 6 metres
   c) 20 metres

7. Which of these is a small tropical fish?
   a) Clownfish
   b) Magicianfish
   c) Builderfish

8. How many legs do crabs have?
   a) Four
   b) Six
   c) Ten

9. What type of creature is a dolphin?
   a) Amphibian
   b) Mammal
   c) Reptile

10. If threatened, a squid might:
    a) Make loud noises
    b) Grow in size
    c) Squirt ink

Help the penguin around the maze until it finds the exit.
See if you are right by flicking to page 103.

MAZE

A E
V
B R
E

R P
O **P** E
O S
I

Word wheels

Can you work out the water animals
in the two word wheels?
See if you are right by flicking to page 103.

Solutions

Crosswords

Page 8–9

Crossword 1

```
D A I S I E S . . S
I . . N . A . . U
F . T . C R U M B
F . Y . O . S . S
I M P O R T A N T
C . I . R . G . A
U N C L E . E . N
L . A . C . . . C
T . L E T T U C E
```

Keyword: TIGER

Crossword 2

```
. C H E R R Y . . .
. U . N . U . R . I
. S E V E N T E E N
. T . E . . L . . T
. O W L S . M A K E
. M . O . . T . . R
. E X P E N S I V E
. R . E . U . V . S
. . . S T R E E T
```

Keyword: PANTHER

Sudokus

Page 10–11

3	6	5	2	1	4
4	1	2	5	6	3
2	3	1	6	4	5
5	4	6	1	3	2
1	2	4	3	5	6
6	5	3	4	2	1

4	3	6	1	5	2
5	2	1	6	4	3
3	6	2	5	1	4
1	4	5	2	3	6
6	5	4	3	2	1
2	1	3	4	6	5

4	2	5	3	1	6
1	3	6	2	4	5
5	4	2	6	3	1
6	1	3	5	2	4
2	6	4	1	5	3
3	5	1	4	6	2

Wordsearches

Page 12–13

```
e k e s u w g f e s
x d a g j a g u a r
o a w s s p o t s s
o p u m a t r l r e
y l i o n r a e e l
u a k t t i r o a r
z z k o h e t p s s
s v c h e e t a h a
t i g e r s a r w e
a x b p l j i d c s
```

```
w a u x l m u p b g
r q c o u g a r s h
a g a t a t s p g g
o p r e d a t o r t
p r n e s c e u i s
e i t o l a n c a
i y h w a l c z r
t l o f m w t e m o
c y r u d s h i h r
f i e r c e a w i a
```

90

Close Up

1 – 6 Tiger   2 – 1 Cheetah   3 – 4 Leopard

4 – 5 Lion   5 – 3 Panther   6 – 2 Puma

Guess what?

1) b – Lion   2) c – Spots   3) a – Puma

4) b – Cheetah   5) c – To help distribute their weight when walking on snow

6) b – Liger   7) c – Tiger   8) c – Pride

9) a – Dense rainforest   10) b – 8 kilometres away

Maze

Word wheels

Cheetah, Jaguar

Solutions

Crosswords

Page 20–21

```
B R E A K F A S T
E       O     O
D E S S E R T   E
S     P   G     S
  B E E H I V E
P   C   V     T
U   V I N E G A R
M   A         E
A P O L O G I S E
```
Keyword: PARROT

```
  C A R R O T S
P   M       E   W
U N P O P U L A R   A R
S   H     E   S   I
H   I     A   C   T
I   B     C   C   E
N E I G H B O U R   S
G   A         P
  A N O T H E R
```
Keyword: SLOTH

Sudokus

Page 22–23

3	6	1	4	2	5
2	4	5	6	1	3
5	1	3	2	4	6
6	2	4	3	5	1
1	3	2	5	6	4
4	5	6	1	3	2

3	5	1	4	6	2
2	6	4	3	1	5
5	3	6	1	2	4
4	1	2	6	5	3
6	2	3	5	4	1
1	4	5	2	3	6

3	4	5	1	2	6
1	2	6	3	4	5
5	1	2	6	3	4
6	3	4	5	1	2
2	6	1	4	5	3
4	5	3	2	6	1

Wordsearches

Page 24–25

```
a g s c o c e l o t
q o t p a n t h e r
c r o c o d i l e p
b u s h b a b y j i
r p a y e t a p i r
t s a y n r b x t a
t o r a n g u t a n
r l m a c a w s z h
t o j a v c o b r a
x c h a m e l e o n
```

```
i m b a t o u c a n
l l a x p h m h g e
m v a e y i l i o n
q y o l t x x m r t
q t p q h u o p i d
a n a c o n d a l u
s l r f n a r n l o
y f r o g a r z i a
s l o t h i s e i p
i s t f o e i e p s
```

92

Page 26-27

Spot the difference

Page 28-29

Guess what?

1) b – Parrot

2) b – Gorilla

3) b – Slow

4) c – More than 3,500

5) b - Colonies

6) a – Their massive beaks

7) a – Green anacondas

8) b – A hoofed mammal

9) a – Cobra

10) c – 45 years

Maze

Word wheels

Gorilla, Piranha

Solutions

Crosswords

D	I	R	E	C	T			
E		E			T		I	
C		C	U	B		R	A	N
E		O		E		I		T
M	A	R	M	A	L	A	D	E
B		D		R		N		R
E	Y	E		D	O	G		N
R		R			L			E
			N	E	W	E	S	T

Keyword: CROCODILE

R	O	U	N	D	E	R	S	
		N		I			T	
O	D	D		S	T	E	A	M
		E		A			I	
A	E	R	O	P	L	A	N	E
	A			P		G		
A	G	R	E	E		A	G	E
	L			A		I		
E	N	T	R	A	N	C	E	

Keyword: OTTER

Sudokus

5	4	1	6	3	2
6	2	3	5	4	1
4	1	6	2	5	3
2	3	5	1	6	4
3	5	2	4	1	6
1	6	4	3	2	5

2	5	4	3	1	6
3	6	1	4	5	2
6	3	5	1	2	4
1	4	2	5	6	3
5	2	3	6	4	1
4	1	6	2	3	5

5	1	3	6	4	2
2	4	6	3	5	1
6	5	4	2	1	3
1	3	2	4	6	5
4	2	5	1	3	6
3	6	1	5	2	4

Wordsearches

94

Spot the difference

Guess what?

1) a – Anaconda   2) a – Crane   3) c – Mallard

4) b – Building dams   5) c – Rat   6) c – Crab

7) b – To lay eggs   8) a – Bog   9) a – Water lily

10) a – Tadpole

Maze

Word wheels

Alligator, Turtle

Solutions

Page 44–45

Crosswords

	A	C	R	O	B	A	T	
H		E		L			E	
E	E	L		R		L	N	
X		E	V	E	N	I	N	G
A		B		P		G	L	
G	O	R	I	L	L	A	A	
O		A		Y		T	E	N
N		T				O	D	
	L	E	O	P	A	R	D	

Keyword: ELEPHANT

	D	E	C	R	E	A	S	E
E		H			U		C	
C	H	O	S	E		B		O
I		C		L	E	M	O	N
S		O		B		A		S
I	G	L	O	O		R		I
O		A		W	E	I	R	D
N		T				N		E
	R	E	I	N	D	E	E	R

Keyword: CHEETAH

Page 46–47

Sudokus

2	3	5	6	4	1
1	4	6	3	5	2
3	5	1	2	6	4
4	6	2	1	3	5
6	1	4	5	2	3
5	2	3	4	1	6

5	3	4	1	6	2
2	1	6	5	3	4
1	4	5	6	2	3
3	6	2	4	1	5
4	2	1	3	5	6
6	5	3	2	4	1

4	1	5	3	6	2
3	6	2	4	1	5
6	2	4	1	5	3
1	5	3	2	4	6
2	4	6	5	3	1
5	3	1	6	2	4

Page 48–49

Wordsearches

e	j	a	c	k	a	l	s	m	g
d	r	r	w	i	l	d	d	o	g
q	r	b	x	b	k	s	j	n	s
f	h	a	o	z	g	r	t	g	o
b	y	b	o	r	o	l	p	o	s
p	e	o	o	l	r	p	h	o	t
r	n	o	y	a	i	j	c	s	r
r	a	n	t	e	l	o	p	e	i
a	g	a	z	e	l	l	e	l	c
i	m	p	a	l	a	t	q	p	h

y	h	l	a	r	l	r	q	r	w
r	t	c	h	e	e	t	a	h	a
i	x	a	l	i	o	n	z	i	r
a	b	e	l	e	p	h	a	n	t
c	z	e	b	r	a	t	u	o	h
f	b	f	l	r	r	o	o	c	o
c	r	o	c	o	d	i	l	e	g
g	i	r	a	f	f	e	y	r	y
p	r	b	u	f	f	a	l	o	a
p	i	o	t	h	v	s	t	s	t

Close Up

1 – 3 Hippo

2 – 2 Giraffe

3 – 5 Roller

4 – 6 Zebra

5 – 4 Rhino

6 – 1 Gazelle

Guess what?

1) a – Zebra

2) b – 52 cm

3) c – Bull

4) b – Spotted hyena

5) b – Five

6) a – Canines

7) a – Antelope

8) c – Crocodile

9) c – Cheetah

10) a – 25 cm

Maze

Word wheels

Buffalo, Gazelle

Solutions

Crosswords

Crossword 1:

F	A	N	T	A	S	T	I	C
A		O		R			R	A
V	A	N		T		I	R	
O		E	X	A	M	P	L	E
U			B				F	
R	E	G	U	L	A	R	U	
I		I		E		A	L	L
T		V		E		I	L	
E	M	E	R	G	E	N	C	Y

Keyword: FARMER

Crossword 2:

	H		D				R	
N	A	T	I	O	N		E	
	L		N		O	N	C	E
	L		O	W	N		T	
C	O	W	S		S	W	A	N
	W		A	P	E		N	
M	E	N	U		N		G	
	E		R	E	S	U	L	T
	N			E			E	

Keyword: TRACTOR

Sudokus

Sudoku 1:

3	6	5	2	1	4
4	1	2	5	6	3
2	3	1	6	4	5
5	4	6	1	3	2
1	2	4	3	5	6
6	5	3	4	2	1

Sudoku 2:

4	3	6	1	5	2
5	2	1	6	4	3
3	6	2	5	1	4
1	4	5	2	3	6
6	5	4	3	2	1
2	1	3	4	6	5

Sudoku 3:

4	2	5	3	1	6
1	3	6	2	4	5
5	4	2	6	3	1
6	1	3	5	2	4
2	6	4	1	5	3
3	5	1	4	6	2

Wordsearches

98

Page 62–63

Close Up

1 – 5 Pig

2 – 1 Goat

3 – 6 Horse

4 – 3 Cow

5 – 4 Sheep

6 – 2 Duck

Page 64–65

Guess what?

1) a –Rooster

2) b – Skein

3) a – Sheep

4) a – Chicken

5) a – Sheepdog

6) c – Stable

7) c – Sheep

8) b – Calf

9) c – Lamb

10) a – Jenny

Maze

Word wheels

Rabbit, Donkey

Solutions

Page 68–69

Crosswords

	T		C		F				
B	R	I	L	L	I	A	N	T	
	U		O		M			O	
M	E	N		C	R	O	W	D	
U		O		K		U		A	
S	T	R	A	W		S	L	Y	
I		M		I				I	
C	L	A	S	S	R	O	O	M	
		L		E				N	

Keyword: MEERKAT

	E		D				Y	
E	X	C	I	T	E		E	
	C		S		L	O	S	E
	E		C		E		T	
A	L	S	O		P	E	E	L
	L		V		H		R	
H	E	R	E		A		D	
N					D			
T		R	U	N	W	A	Y	

Keyword: OSTRICH

Page 70–71

Sudokus

4	5	6	3	2	1
2	1	3	6	5	4
5	4	1	2	6	3
6	3	2	1	4	5
1	6	4	5	3	2
3	2	5	4	1	6

3	6	4	5	1	2
2	1	5	4	3	6
6	2	1	3	4	5
4	5	3	6	2	1
5	3	2	1	6	4
1	4	6	2	5	3

5	6	4	3	2	1
1	3	2	4	5	6
4	5	3	1	6	2
6	2	1	5	3	4
2	1	5	6	4	3
3	4	6	2	1	5

Page 72–73

Wordsearches

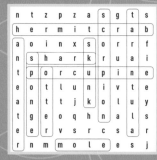

```
n t z p z a s g t s
h e r m i t c r a b
a o i n x s o r r f
n s h a r k r u a i
t p o r c u p i n e
e o t l u n i v t e
a n t t j k o l u y
t g e o q h n a l s
e e r v s r c s a r
r n m m o l e s j
```

```
u h r f i t r e z m
a t b s n h q l p b
v h a x a i m n e s
o d d a v t q p n o
w o l f a k e e g i
l l e m u r a a u b
g p a n d a c i s
c h a m e l e o n q
l i o s t r i c h t
l n p m e e r k a t
```

Spot the difference

Guess what?

1) a – Chameleon   2) a – Madagascar

3) b – To make it hard for predators to detect them

4) b – Its sharp spines   5) a – Emits a foul-smelling spray

6) a – Using their sticky tongues

7) c – 800   8) b – Up to four minutes

9) c – Bamboo   10) b – In groups

Maze

Word wheels

Dolphin, Penguin

Solutions

Crosswords

Crossword 1 grid:

```
C U D D L E
A   I       A   F
R   S U M   C A R
E   A   E   C   I
L I G H T N I N G
E   R   A   D   H
S E E   L I E   T
S   E       N   E
    K I T T E N
```

Keyword: STARFISH

Crossword 2 grid:

```
D I S T A N C E
    H   M     R
E A R   B E A R S
    E   U     O
J E W E L L E R Y
    R   A   A
Q U E E N   R A T
    P   C   T
    T O G E T H E R
```

Keyword: OCTOPUS

Sudokus

1	6	4	2	5	3
3	5	2	4	6	1
2	4	6	3	1	5
5	1	3	6	4	2
6	3	1	5	2	4
4	2	5	1	3	6

5	3	1	6	2	4
4	6	2	1	5	3
2	5	4	3	1	6
6	1	3	5	4	2
1	4	6	2	3	5
3	2	5	4	6	1

6	1	2	3	4	5
3	5	4	1	6	2
1	2	3	4	5	6
5	4	6	2	3	1
4	6	1	5	2	3
2	3	5	6	1	4

Wordsearches

Wordsearch 1:

```
o t r s q u i d k f
j s t a r f i s h t
j e l l y f i s h u
s a r d i n e m u a
a h q g x i b r w p
l o c t o p u s b o
m r r t r o u t t p
o s e a w e e d s t
n e l l s j h l e h
x i u z r c o r a l
```

Wordsearch 2:

```
r c f p j s t g t u
p s r o e l u r o p
g h i i e r n s y i
g a l l i g a t o r
t r o o a x r u g a
x k b e a v e r r n
i o s o t c e t v n
o u t x y r e l p a
l k e w h a l e g j
l r r t z b p h u f
```

Spot the difference

Guess what?

1) a – 35 mph
2) c – Eight
3) c – 13 metres
4) b – Five
5) c – Reptile
6) b – 6 metres
7) a – Clownfish
8) c – Ten
9) b – Mammal
10) c – Squirt ink

Maze

Word wheels

Beaver, Porpoise

Look for more puzzle books in this series!

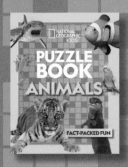

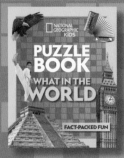